T0165094

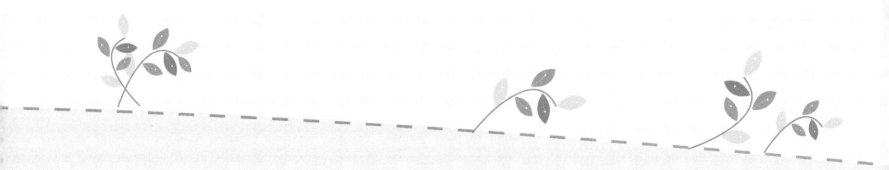

The Most Beautiful
Gusu Fairy Tales

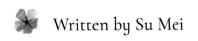 Written by Su Mei

 Illustrated by Rui Ling

The Butterfly Kite at the Taihu Lake

Books Beyond Boundaries

ROYAL COLLINS

Interpreting Suzhou's Culture through Fairy Tale Picture Books

WANG QUANGEN

Chinese people are familiar with the saying, "Suzhou and Hangzhou are the heavens on earth."

Suzhou, a beautiful city with a rich culture of 2,500 years, has been an aesthetic inspiration throughout history. Still, depicting Suzhou's culture through illustrated fairy tales was unprecedented. Therefore, Soochow University Press invited Su Mei, a well-known local children's writer, and Rui Ling, an experienced illustrator, to co-create this book series. Aside from its pioneering role in this subject area, it is also the first "cultural picture book" series to combine Chinese elements, regional cultures, ethnic expressions, and fairy tale fantasies. For these reasons, I fell deeply in love with the books' words and images the moment I saw them.

Su Mei has a brilliant imagination and an exquisite style—she is a superb writer. Choosing a topic and putting it into words is a great challenge given Suzhou's colorful and diverse regional culture. Applying the method of time travel in fairy tale writing, Su Mei lets Meiduo'er, an old cat who has been away from Suzhou for a long time, fly back home out of concern for Tiancizhuang, which will soon be pulled down. With the help of a little girl, Nannan, she begins a journey to find her childhood friends ...

Through Meiduo'er's eyes, the author focused on elements that embody the most regional characteristics of Suzhou: river towns, gardens, Taihu Lake, embroidery, ginkgo trees, local snacks, the dialect, and silk. Each element is exemplified in a story; altogether, the stories connect Suzhou's regional cultures and customs effectively. By reading them, children can learn more about Suzhou.

Although the city's beauty is hard to delineate with lines and colors, illustrator Rui Ling did an excellent job in making the works vivid, engaging, and diverse.

I sincerely offer my congratulations on the publication of *The Most Beautiful Gusu Fairy Tales*. I hope that all children can benefit from Suzhou's splendid landscape and glorious culture.

WANG QUANGEN is a professor and doctoral advisor at the School of Chinese Language and Literature of Beijing Normal University, vice president of the Children's Literature Committee of the China Writers Association, and director of the China Children's Literature Education Research Center. He is also vice president of the Asia Children's Literature Research Academy, deputy director of the Professional Committee of Chinese Language Teaching in Chinese Contemporary Literature Research, and review expert of The National Social Science Fund of China. As a distinguished academic, he enjoys a special government allowance for life.

About the Writer:

SU MEI is a member of the China Writers Association and director of the China Society for the Studies of Children's Literature. She now teaches at Soochow University. Su has published over six hundred fairy tales and more than sixty story collections. Her math and science fairy tale picture books have been exported to Singapore, Malaysia, Thailand, Indonesia, and other countries. Many of her works have been selected for Chinese textbooks for kindergartens and US elementary schools. Su is the winner of many awards, including the "Second China Children's Book Gold Award," "Bing Xin Children's Literature Award," "Bing Xin Children's Book Award," and second place in the "First Sina Flash Fairy Tale Competition."

About the Illustrator:

ZHANG RUILING is a professional illustrator and picture book painter. Born in Heze, Shandong Province, Zhang studied at the Department of Design at Shandong College of Art and the Department of Photography at Beijing Film Academy. Her published works include *I Have a Date with Zhuangzi*, etc. Zhang was the winner of the "2012 Bing Xin Children's Book Award."

The Dragon Boat Festival was approaching, and Granny was preparing the *zongzi* (a kind of dumpling) with bamboo leaves, sticky rice, and dates.

枫桥夜泊

月落乌 tí shuāng 满天

江枫 yú 火对 chóu 眠

姑苏城外 hán 山寺

yè 半钟 shēng 到客船

Meiduo'er remembered that she and Awang used to pick reed leaves at Taihu Lake. Will Awang be there now?

She stood up and said, "I want to go for a walk along Taihu Lake."

"I'll go too," said Nannan.

They got on the flying carpet and soon arrived at Taihu Lake.

They stopped by Taihu Lake and enjoyed the beautiful view.

The water was wide and covered in shining waves. They saw white sails and mountains in the distance. Waterfowl sometimes flew by.

Some fishing boats were starting the day's work.
The fishermen sang happily as they set sail.

Meiduo'er and Nannan continued their walk and saw the crab farms.

Then, they saw the pearl farms.

Meiduo'er bought a pearl necklace at a street fair, and Nannan bought pearl powder for her granny.

They walked into the reeds and picked some leaves.

"Granny can use these for the *zongzi* next time!" said Meiduo'er.

When they got tired, they sat down on some rocks to rest.

"Ouch!" Meiduo'er suddenly cried out. A little crab had caught her tail with his claws.

"Please don't hurt me! I'll not eat you," said Meiduo'er.

"I'm sorry. I thought you were here to catch us," said the little crab.

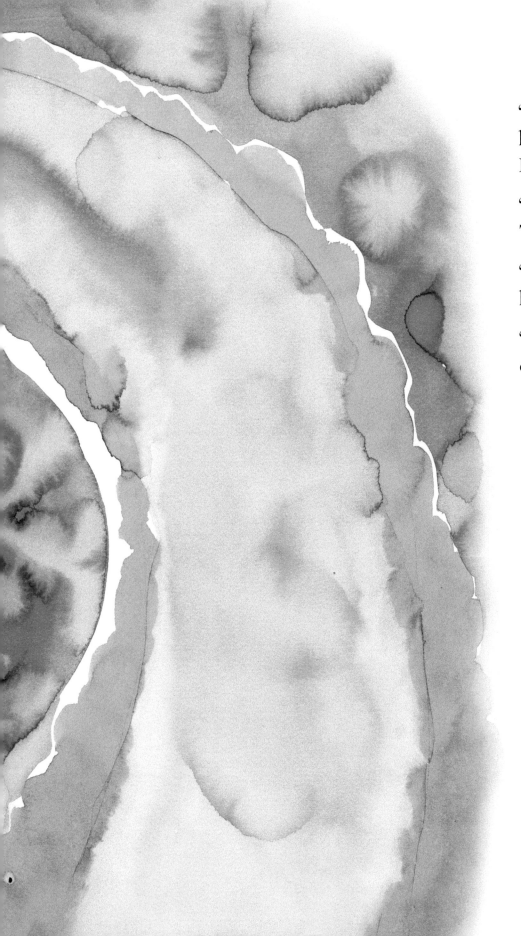

"Have you seen a little yellow dog here?" asked Mei Duo'er. "Oh, no. He's not so little anymore."

"There are many yellow dogs here. They all live here."

"Awang doesn't live here. He comes here for a visit."

"Then I don't know," said the little crab, and he returned to the water.

Just then, a butterfly kite flew by, and two boys followed.

"My kite flew away!" one of them cried, "My grandpa made it for me. I can't lose it, or my mom will be mad!"

"Why don't you ask your grandpa to make another one?" asked Nannan.

"Jie's grandpa passed away," said the other boy.

"Oh, I'm so sorry!" said Nannan.

"Don't worry! I'll get it back for you."

With that said, Meiduo'er took out the flying carpet and murmured, "Lock the gold and silver locks, unfold the gold and silver carpets. Avoid the mountains, away from the eagles, and get the kite ahead."

The flying carpet took Meiduo'er up after the kite.

"Can she do it?" asked Jie.

"Of course! Just wait," said Nannan.

They began to chat.

The boy who lost his kite was called Jie. His mother had a shop on Embroidery Street in Zhenhu, a district in Suzhou. The other boy was Maomao. Both his parents were embroidery workers.

"Your father can do embroidery, too?"

"What's so strange about that? Many men in Zhenhu can do embroidery. Many families bought houses and cars because of their work."

Just then, Meiduo'er returned with the kite.

"Wow, you did it! What a wonderful carpet! Thank you! Thank you so much!" said Jie.

"Please come home with me. I'll treat you to some of this year's good Biluochun tea (a famous green tea grown around Suzhou)," said Jie.

"Thank you, but we need to go somewhere else today. We'll visit you some other time." Meiduo'er waved them goodbye.

Knowledge Station

Taihu Lake is the largest inland lake in the coastal area of eastern China and the third-largest freshwater lake in China. Two-thirds of the lake is in the city of Suzhou.

Taihu Lake is rich in aquatic products. People often say, "There are countless fish and prawns in its 800 miles of water." The lake is famous for its "three whites": icefish, white fish, and white prawns.

Starting the day's work with the sun at Taihu Lake

In 1982, Taihu Lake was included in the first batch of national scenic spots by the China State Council as the "Jiangsu Taihu Lake Scenic Area."

Reeds at Taihu Lake

The famous attractions include the Suzhou Qiyuan Garden, Yonghui Temple, Xuanyang Cave, Biyun Cave, Yuwang Temple, Baima Temple, Luohan Temple, Sheng'en Temple, East and West Mountain Scenic Spots, Sanyuan Cultural Spot, Suzhou Taihu National Tourism Resort, Suzhou Taihu Wetland Park, Suzhou Taihu Park, Shigong Mountain, Sanshan Island, Piaomiao Peak, Linwu Cave, Diaohua Building, and Xiangxuehai.

On October 25, 1994, the Taihu Bridge, the longest bridge in China's inland lakes, was officially opened to traffic.

The Taihu Bridge connects the Yuyang Mountain in Xukou, Wuzhong District, Suzhou City in the east, and the west Dongting Mountain in the west. It consists of three bridges, crossing the Changsha and Yeshan Islands. It is 4,308 meters (about 2.68 miles) long and 12 meters wide, with 181 bridge openings.

🌿 Taihu Bridge

🌿 Imperial Pier of Qiyuan Garden at East Mountain

The Taihu pearl is one of nine major pearl varieties in China. Nowadays, most Taihu pearls are artificially bred. These freshwater pearls are lustrous, full, and smooth. They are also known for their outstanding shape, hardness, proportion, elasticity, and overall quality, making them both precious decorations and medicinal materials.

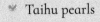 Taihu pearls

Late autumn and early winter are the times when Taihu crabs mature. These big, heavy crabs with "blue shell, white belly, golden claws, yellow hair" are extremely delicious for their rich, tender meat.

Nannan's Stories

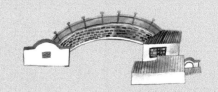

The Legend of Taihu White Fish

The Taihu white fish is also known as the "silver knife" because of its touching story.

When the Qing army troops invaded Taihu Lake at the end of the Ming Dynasty (1368–1644), a fisherman called Zhang San and his compatriots fought back vigorously. During a battle, he was shot in the arm by an arrow, and his sword fell into the water. Despite the great pain, he did not withdraw. Instead, he picked up a silver knife from the lake and waved at the enemies.

The Qing soldiers were shocked by his gallantry, and they ran away. When Zhang San looked again, he saw what he had in his hand was a shining white fish. After they learned this story, people began to refer to the Taihu white fish as the "silver knife."

The Legend of Taihu

Long, long ago, on the Heavenly Queen Mother's birthday, the Jade Emperor sent her a huge silver bowl with 72 giant emerald and colorful jade fish and birds.

When the party started, the Monkey King, who was not invited, made havoc in heaven and smashed everything he saw. The huge silver bowl also fell off and crashed into a giant lake, which became the Taihu Lake of today. The 72 emeralds changed into 72 mountains, the jade fish changed into icefish, and the jade birds changed into mandarin ducks.

The Most Beautiful Gusu Fairy Tales:
The Butterfly Kite at the Taihu Lake

Written by Su Mei
Illustrated by Rui Ling
Translated by Wu Meilian

First published in 2024 by Royal Collins Publishing Group Inc.
Groupe Publication Royal Collins Inc.
BKM Royalcollins Publishers Private Limited

Headquarters: 550-555 boul. René-Lévesque O Montréal (Québec)
H2Z1B1 Canada
India office: 805 Hemkunt House, 8th Floor, Rajendra Place, New
Delhi 110 008

Original Edition © Soochow University Press

ISBN: 978-1-4878-1186-0

To find out more about our publications,
please visit www.royalcollins.com.